THE OLYMP
MODERN OLYMPIC GAMES

HAYDN MIDDLETON

The Olympic spirit

The modern Olympic Games began in 1896. Since then the Games' organizers have tried to ensure that every competitor keeps to the true Olympic spirit. This spirit is based on fair play, international friendship, a love of sport purely for its own sake and the ideal that it is more important to take part than to win.

Heinemann
LIBRARY

First published in Great Britain by Heinemann Library,
Halley Court, Jordan Hill, Oxford OX2 8EJ,
a division of Reed Educational and Professional Publishing Ltd.
Heinemann is a registered trademark of Reed Educational & Professional Publishing Limited.

OXFORD MELBOURNE AUCKLAND
JOHANNESBURG BLANTYRE GABORONE
IBADAN PORTSMOUTH NH (USA) CHICAGO

Designed by AMR
Originated by Dot Gradations
Printed in Hong Kong/China

04 03 02 01 00
10 9 8 7 6 5 4 3 2 1

ISBN 0 431 05924 1
This title is also available in a hardback library edition (ISBN 0 431 05919 5)

British Library Cataloguing in Publication Data
Middleton, Haydn
  Modern olympic games. – (The olympics)
  1.Olympic Games – Juvenile literature 2.Olympics – Records
  – Juvenile literature
  I.Title.
  796.4·8

Acknowledgements
The Publishers would like to thank the following for permission to reproduce photographs:
Allsport: pp4, 6, 7, 8, 9, 11 (left), 12, 13, 14, 15, 17, 18, 19, 20, 22, 24, 25, 26, 27; Colorsport:
pp11 (right), 23, 28, 29; Corbis: Nik Wheeeler p16; Michael Holford: p5.

Cover photograph reproduced with permission of Sporting Pictures (UK) Ltd.

Every effort has been made to contact copyright holders of any material reproduced in this
book. Any omissions will be rectified in subsequent printings if notice is given to the Publisher.

For more information about Heinemann Library books, or to order, please phone
++44 (0)1865 888066, or send a fax to ++44 (0)1865 314091. You can visit our website
at www.heinemann.co.uk.

Any words appearing in the text in bold, **like this**, are explained in the Glossary.

Contents

Introduction

The Olympic Games are the most important international athletic competition in the world. Every four years they bring together thousands of the world's best athletes, to compete in an ever-growing number of individual and team sports. Millions of spectators have been lucky enough to attend the Games and marvel at the astounding performances. Over a billion TV viewers world-wide now tune in too, and share in the excitement as it happens. This book tells the story of how the Games began and how they have developed – way beyond the expectations of their founders – into the competition we know today.

A Games like no other

Since the first modern Games in 1896, the Olympics have been held in seventeen different countries on four different continents. And since 1924, there have been separate Winter Olympics as well as those held in the summer. Countless sportsmen and women all over the world have focused their hopes, dreams and talents on taking part in these Games and – maybe, just maybe – achieving the ultimate success by winning an Olympic gold medal. Many have not been able to fulfil this ambition – but no one who competes at an Olympic Games can forget the experience. As this book shows, each Games has its own atmosphere and flavour, depending on where it is held. Yet every Games also has traditional rituals and ceremonies, which makes the whole occasion uniquely Olympic.

'I do not know why man likes sport,' wrote American author Ed Wheeler in a book written for the Atlanta Olympic Games in 1996. 'Maybe for the same reason that the dog tosses his bone. Is it a statement of possession, amusement or boredom? The Olympics are, or could be, the highest expression of sport. At core, and in the nations, the Olympics test our bonds to earth and lift the fact that we are alive.'

At times, as you will find, the Games have faced serious political crises. On several occasions, during major wars, they have not been held. People have often predicted a complete end to the Games, which can be so difficult – and expensive – to organize. Yet they have not only survived – they have *grown* in popularity and scale. The Millennium Games, due to be held in Sydney, Australia, in the year 2000, will feature more competitors than any previous Games.

Olympic origins

Although the modern Games began in 1896, they were not the first Olympics ever. For those, you have to go back almost 3000 years – to ancient Greece. The five-day-long Games held then featured running, combat sports, the **pentathlon**, horse-riding and chariot races.

We have records of winners dating back to 776BC but the ancient Games came to an end in AD393, when the Roman Emperor, Theodosius I, banned all non-Christian worship throughout his empire. Since the Olympics were held in honour of the Greek gods, they had to come to an end as well. But just over 1500 years later, they began again in their modern form. Turn over and find out how it happened....

This ancient Greek vase painting shows the old Greek sport of *pankration* – man-to-man combat in which almost any form of aggression was allowed.

Bring back the Games!

The Games did not start again of their own accord. By the end of the 19th century, plenty of people in Europe and America were keen on sport. Some might even have dreamed of a brand new global Games, based on the ancient Greek Olympics. But one man above all others made this dream come true. His name was Pierre de Fredi, Baron de Coubertin, a French **aristocrat** who was not particularly good at sport himself!

A religion of sport

De Coubertin (1863–1937) was a widely travelled man. In Britain he saw how important sport was in the **public schools**. In the USA he admired the highly developed training and coaching programmes at the colleges. Sport became a kind of religion to him – as you can see from what he said and wrote about it:

Baron Pierre de Coubertin, father of the modern Olympic Games.

Through sport, he believed, 'our body rises above its animal nature'. Sporting contests were 'the means of bringing to perfection the strong and hopeful youth … helping towards the perfection of all human society'. 'Sport' he concluded, 'should allow man to know himself, to control himself and to conquer himself.' (Only *man*, you will notice, not woman. Like the ancient Greeks, and most other people of his own time, de Coubertin thought a woman's place was in the home, not the stadium.)

From 1892, he set about trying to convert others to his strong faith in sport. His aim was to set up some Games where the 'youth of the world' could come together in peaceful, character-building competition: a modern Olympics. It was especially important to him that everyone taking part should be **amateur**. The glory of being an Olympian, not money, would be the athletes' reward.

Birth of an 'Olympic family'

It might seem surprising now, but at first de Coubertin found little support for his grand idea. Then in June 1894, at a congress in Paris, he persuaded **delegates** from twelve countries to back his plan to revive the Olympics. The Games would be held in Athens, the capital of Greece, in 1896. Then, at four-yearly intervals, they would be hosted by other major cities. Soon more countries came into this new 'Olympic family', and an International Olympic Committee (IOC) was set up to organize and oversee the Games. De Coubertin himself was chairman of the IOC for 30 years.

The first modern Olympic Games were duly held in Athens over ten days in June 1896. An estimated 245 men – most of them Greek – took part in 43 events. Few of the performances were brilliant. In fact, in events like the discus and long jump, champions from ancient times may well have achieved greater distances! But the Games were hugely popular with the big crowds that came to watch. The world's appetite had been whetted.

This was the official report of the 1896 Games. Athletes from fourteen different nations took part.

The Olympic Charter's Article 46 states that 'the Olympic Games are not competitions between nations'. They are contests between individuals and teams. But ever since 1896, nations have competed against one another for the most sporting success.

ΟΛΥΜΠΙΆΚΟΙ ΑΓΩΝΕΣ

ATHÈNES 1896

JEUX OLYMPIQUES

The Games roll on: 1900-36

		COMPETITORS		NATIONS	EVENTS
		Men	Women		
II	1900 Paris, France	1206	19	26	87
III	1904 St Louis, USA	681	6	13	94
IV	1908 London, UK	1999	36	22	109
V	1912 Stockholm, Sweden	2490	57	28	102
VI	1916 Berlin, Germany	Cancelled because of World War One			
VII	1920 Antwerp, Belgium	2591	78	29	154
VIII	1924 Paris, France	2956	136	44	126
IX	1928 Amsterdam, Netherlands	2724	290	46	109
X	1932 Los Angeles, USA	1281	127	37	116
XI	1936 Berlin, Germany	3738	328	49	129

Dates: 20 May–28 Oct; 1 July–23 Nov; 27 Apr–31 Oct; 29 June–22 July; 20 Apr–12 Sept; 4 May–27 July; 17 May–12 Aug; 30 July–14 Aug; 1–16 August.

The table above shows how the Olympic story continued in the 40 years after 1896. As time went on, the Games were organized over a shorter and shorter period. For the earlier Games, the word *disorganized* was closer to the truth. Some competitors were not even aware that the event they were taking part in was part of the Olympic Games. Sometimes, too, **professional** sportsmen were allowed to compete.

Slowly but surely organization improved, and there were fewer disputes over which events were official and which were not. The fifth Games at Stockholm set a new standard for efficiency – but then the 1916 Games never took place, because of World War One. In ancient Greece this would not have happened. Back then, a **truce** was declared – to let the athletes travel to the Games and compete in safety.

The official Olympic poster advertising the 1912 Games – the first at which nations from all five continents took part.

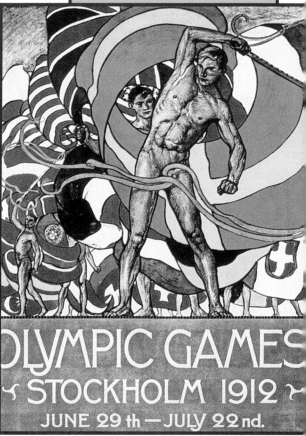

OLYMPIC GAMES
STOCKHOLM 1912
JUNE 29th — JULY 22nd.

Games between the wars

The Olympics resumed in 1920. The Games were held in Belgium, which had suffered horribly during World War One. 'All this is quite nice,' remarked the Belgian King at the opening ceremony, 'but it certainly lacks people.' The 1924 Games in Paris had bigger crowds, but trouble kept breaking out because the fans were so aggressive in their support – definitely not in the 'Olympic spirit'.

The men's 4 × 400 m relay at the Berlin Olympics of 1936 – the first to be shown on television. Berliners could watch the Games for free on giant screens in the city's theatres.

Women participated in **track and field** events for the first time at the 1928 Games in Amsterdam. Before then they had taken part in tennis, golf, archery, figure skating, yachting and fencing. At the next Games, in Los Angeles, fewer women *and* men competed. This was partly because it was too expensive for many Europeans to travel to the faraway USA. At that time, making and selling alcohol

was against the American law. But the athletes from France and Italy were allowed to drink wine – because they said it was a vital part of their diet!

In 1931 the International Olympic Committee decided to stage the eleventh Games in Germany. Two years later Hitler and his **Nazi** Party came to power. Despite much protest, the 1936 Games went ahead in Berlin. As a spectacle they were lavish, since Hitler wanted to prove to the world the 'supremacy' of the German people. Again, this was far from the true Olympic spirit. Hitler's influence over the Olympic story extended beyond 1936, when World War Two led to a cancellation of the Games until 1948.

Truly global Olympics: 1948-68

		COMPETITORS		NATIONS	EVENTS
		Men	Women		
XII and XIII 1940 and 1944	Cancelled because of World War Two				
XIV 1948 London, UK	29 July–14 Aug	3714	385	59	136
XV 1952 Helsinki, Finland	19 July–3 Aug	4407	518	69	149
XVI 1956 Melbourne, Australia	22 Nov– 8 Dec	2958	384	72	151
XVII 1960 Rome, Italy	25 Aug–11 Sept	4738	610	83	150
XVIII 1964 Tokyo, Japan	10–24 October	4457	683	93	163
XIX 1968 Mexico City, Mexico	12–27 October	4750	781	112	172

During the 20 years from 1948 to 1968, more and more nations took part in the Olympics. The number of events grew too – until in 1968 there were 172 of them, in sports ranging from athletics and **equestrianism** to yachting and shooting. Each Games produced brilliant performances and fantastic champions who soon became household names all around the world. But there were troubles too – partly because the Games could not remain entirely separate from events in the world around them.

War by other means

The British did a good job of hosting the 1948 Games in the wake of World War Two. The countries defeated in that war, Germany and Japan, were not invited to take part – just as the losers of World War One were kept out of the 1920 Games. Some countries that had recently become **Communist** also sent teams to compete. From this moment on, rivalry between Communist and non-Communist nations would be a major feature of the Olympic Games.

The most powerful Communist nation of all – the Soviet Union (**USSR**) – joined the Olympics for the highly exciting 1952 Games in Finland. Afterwards, the official Soviet newspaper claimed the USSR had 'won' the Games, and thus shown the 'world superiority' of Soviet athletes. The USSR's great **Cold War** rival, the USA, responded that its own athletes had 'won'.

Broader horizons

In 1956, the Olympics were first staged in the southern hemisphere. Several nations – including Egypt, Iraq, Holland and Spain – refused to send teams to these Games in Melbourne, Australia. That was their way of showing disgust at political or military **aggression** carried out by other competing nations. There were to be more such **boycotts** in the future. The International Olympic Committee (IOC) itself banned a nation from taking part in the 1960 Games in Rome: South Africa, as a punishment for its brutal treatment of non-white peoples. The ban lasted for 32 years, by which time this system of **apartheid** had ended.

The Games then made their debut in Asia when Tokyo expertly hosted the 1964 Games. But there were fierce disputes when the IOC announced Mexico City as the venue for 1968. It was more than 2000 metres above sea level, and according to one Danish newspaper: 'At least half a year is needed to adapt to the oxygen-poor air. One's life would be endangered trying to break records.' In the event, records *were* broken there but no one died. Another controversy arose when women athletes were asked to take sex-tests. This was because some competitors were suspected of using chemicals to 'improve' their bodies – effectively making themselves male!

Two Olympic opening ceremonies: at London in 1948 and – rather more spectacularly – at Tokyo in 1964.

Towards 2000: the Games since 1972

			COMPETITORS		NATIONS	EVENTS
			Men	Women		
XX	1972 Munich, West Germany	26 Aug–10 Sept	6065	1058	121	195
XXI	1976 Montreal, Canada	17 July–1 Aug	4781	1247	92	198
XXII	1980 Moscow, USSR	19 July–3 Aug	4092	1125	80	203
XXIII	1984 Los Angeles, USA	28 July–12 Aug	5230	1567	140	221
XXIV	1988 Seoul, South Korea	17 Sept–2 Oct	6279	2186	159	237
XXV	1992 Barcelona, Spain	24 July–9 Aug	6659	2708	169	257
XXVI	1996 Atlanta, USA	19 July–4 Aug	6797	3513	197	271

At the first Games in 1896, sportsmen from fourteen nations took part. A century later, at the Atlanta Games, men and women of almost 200 nations competed. The Olympic motto is 'Swifter, Higher, Stronger'. But when it came to hosting the Games, it might have been changed to 'Bigger, Dearer, Tougher'. The Germans spent $30 million on staging the 1936 Games. When the Olympics returned to Germany in 1972, at Munich, they cost almost *70* times that amount. And although those Games were a great sporting success, disaster still struck when Palestinian **terrorists** caused the deaths of eleven Israeli athletes.

The 1976 Games in Canada were hit by two different problems. Firstly many African nations stayed away because New Zealand, an Olympic nation, had played the banned South Africans (see previous page) at rugby union. Secondly, through bad planning, the Games proved massively expensive to the **taxpayers** of host city Montreal.

The awesome stadium complex built for the 1972 Games at Munich.

More world records were broken at the 1980 Games in Moscow than four years earlier in Montreal, but even fewer nations sent teams. This was due to the biggest-ever Olympic **boycott**, led by the USA and including 64 other nations, in protest at the **USSR's** invasion of Afghanistan in 1979. Four years later the USSR led a smaller boycott of sixteen nations for the 1984 Games in Los Angeles, USA, blaming worries about security and '**commercialization**', although many felt that it was revenge for the 1980 boycott. For the first time since 1896 private individuals, not taxpayers, were organizing and paying for these Games. As a result of raising huge sums of money from selling TV rights, tickets and commercial sponsorships there was no danger of another Montreal-style fiasco.

The Millennium beckons

In 1988 the Olympic spotlight shifted to Asia: the 1988 Games were staged in Seoul, South Korea, the so-called 'Land of Morning Calm'. The peaceful efficiency of these Games was scarred by only a small boycott. More worrying for the Olympic movement were the ten athletes disqualified for the illegal use of drugs – three of them gold medallists.

The 1992 and 1996 Games were free of trouble except, tragically, for a terrorist bomb which killed two people in Atlanta.

The 27th Olympic Games are due to be held in Sydney, Australia, in the year 2000. The number of sportsmen and women competing in the Millennium Games will probably be the biggest ever. More than 1.3 million visitors are expected to attend as well. But how does a city win the right to host the Games? Turn over and find out.

Ex-Olympic champion boxer Muhammad Ali lights the Olympic flame at Atlanta, 1996. The opening ceremony entertained 3.5 billion viewers world-wide.

Who gets the Games?

It has always been a great honour to host the Olympic Games. It has also been a very complicated and – increasingly – expensive business to stage them. Greece, the host country of the first modern Games in 1896, wanted them to be staged there permanently. This suggestion was made again in the 1980s, since the cost of organizing each new Games had become so huge for the cities involved.

Both times, the International Olympic Committee (IOC) said no: the Olympic Games are truly international, and should therefore be staged all over the world. An added attraction of this is that a Games held in, say, Tokyo has a very different feel and flavour to one held in Mexico City.

Presidents of the International Olympic Committee

1894–96	Demetrius Vikelas (Greece)
1896–1925	Baron Pierre de Coubertin (France)
1925–42	Count Henri de Baillet-Latour (Belgium)
1946–52	J Sigfrid Edstrom (Sweden)
1952–72	Avery Brundage (USA)
1972–80	Lord Killanin (Ireland)
1980–	Juan Antonio Samaranch (Spain)

The IOC's early rules said that the President should come from the next nation to host the Games. Since Paris was due to host the 1900 Games, that was how de Coubertin got the job in 1896. But then he was persuaded to stay in office until 1925 – and after that he became honorary president until his death in 1937. The IOC, based in Lausanne, Switzerland, is the ruling body of the Olympic Movement. It works closely with the International Federations (IFs) which govern individual Olympic sports and the National Olympic Committees (NOCs) of individual countries. The IOC also chooses the organizing committees which, every four years, have to make sure that the Games run smoothly, fairly and excitingly.

The Olympic Charter

The Olympic Charter is the official set of rules for the Olympic Movement. It says that some of the IOC's aims are: 'to encourage the organization and development of sports and sports competitions; ... to fight against any form of discrimination affecting the Olympic Movement; to lead the fight against doping in sport ... and to see to it that the Olympic Games are held in conditions which demonstrate a responsible concern for environmental issues.'

Best bidder wins

Host cities need a long 'lead-in' time to prepare for the Games. As early as September 1993 Sydney, Australia, was given the go-ahead to stage the Games in the year 2000. But it had to face stiff competition from other big cities.

The IOC has to think carefully about many factors before deciding which bid will be successful. Sydney was helped by the fact that no Games had been held in the southern hemisphere since 1956, and that it has no history of **terrorism**. The bid also made a commitment to host a 'Green Games'. Now, as part of its preparations, Homebush Bay – a neglected **landfill** site that was once called 'the most polluted place in Australia' – is being **reclaimed**. And when a rare colony of green and golden bellfrogs was discovered in the area planned for the Olympic tennis courts, the plans were simply changed and the tennis courts moved!

In 1999 a scandal broke when it was revealed that, in recent times, several cities – including Sydney – had bribed IOC officials to vote for their bids. A major investigation followed, in an attempt to 'clean up' the bidding process and to restore the good name of the IOC.

In 1993 these delegates from Sydney, Australia, celebrated their winning bid to stage the 2000 Olympics in their home city.

The Olympic stadium at Sydney, where the 27th Games will be held in the year 2000.

Global village

A tidal wave of competitors and team officials will arrive in Sydney for the 27th Games in the year 2000. Where will they all stay? The city's organizing committee claims that for the first time in modern Olympic history, they will *all* live in one 'Olympic village' and will be able to walk to their events.

Village or mini-city?

At the earliest modern Games, athletes and officials made do with whatever quarters they could find. The American team of 1912 just stayed on board the liner that had brought them across the ocean to Stockholm. Competitors in Antwerp in 1920 lived in the city's schools – sleeping eight to a classroom!

But at the Los Angeles Games of 1932, the first special Olympic village was built. It was more like a mini-city with its own post office, hospital, fire station and security guards. The guards had instructions to admit no women. There were only 127 female competitors and *they* all stayed in a Los Angeles hotel. A village was also built for the Berlin Games of 1936, and at Helsinki in 1952 there were two – because the **USSR**-led **Communist** countries demanded separate secure quarters for their competitors, partly for fear that they might **defect** to the West.

Part of the Olympic village for the 1996 Games in Atlanta, USA. The organizers of these Olympics called them 'the largest, peacetime social event in human history'.

The building of more recent Olympic villages has helped make host cities better places for their own citizens to live in. In order to erect a village for the Barcelona Games of 1992, a whole stretch of the waterfront was **reclaimed** and developed. Then, after the Games, local people moved into the specially built low-rise apartments and made them their homes.

The design of the village for the 2000 Games in Sydney is extremely **eco-friendly** – featuring solar street-lighting and the recycling of waste for garden irrigation. 'As the 2000 Games are the first major event of the next century,' say the organizers, 'it is fitting that the Olympic Movement leads the push to protect the environment.'

By 1992 **professional** players were allowed to take part in many Olympic events. The United States' basketball 'Dream Team' led by 'Magic' Johnson at the Barcelona Games contained eleven multi-millionaires. Being such superstars, they bypassed the Olympic village and stayed in $900-a-night hotel suites elsewhere in Barcelona. Not quite in the true Olympic spirit?

Village life

Judo silver-medallist Nicola Fairbrother lived in the Olympic village at Barcelona in 1992. 'You can taste the apprehension in the air,' she wrote afterwards, 'sense the hopes and the dreams. All the food in the village was free. You could eat when, and as much as, you liked. Soon the main food hall became like a magnet for socializing.

'I also have vivid memories of the atmosphere walking about the village. It was like a bond that existed through every competitor in the village, regardless of colour, size, shape or sport. You could watch African runners lope by, followed by a group of tiny, Hungarian gymnasts and the Chinese volleyball team and there would be the same look in all of their faces. Everyone in the village seemed united by the incredible experience, everyone seemed *alive*.'

The marathon: ancient meets modern

The longest Olympic race is the marathon. It has been a highlight of the men's programme of events in all the modern Games, and since 1984 there has been a women's marathon too. The idea for the race came from an old Greek legend. In 490BC the Greeks won a famous victory over the Persians at the Battle of Marathon. It was said that Pheidipiddes, a **professional** runner, then rushed the enormous distance of about 40 kilometres back to Athens to break the good news. 'Be joyful, we win!' he declared on arriving – and then dropped dead of exhaustion. Whether the story was true or not, the organizers of the 1896 Games in Athens decided to hold a long-distance race named after the great battle.

Local hero

The first Olympic marathon was 40 kilometres (25 miles) long. Although it was run mainly on roads outside Athens, it was due to finish in the Olympic stadium. To the joy of the huge crowd waiting there, the first man home was local farmer Spiridon Louis, in a time of 2 hours 58 minutes 50 seconds. It was Greece's only victory at the Games and local merchants tried to shower Louis with gifts. All he accepted was a horse and cart to transport water to his village.

Spiridon Louis, the first Olympic marathon winner in 1896. Forty years later, the German Olympic Organizing Committee brought him to Berlin for the 1936 Games. There he presented to German leader Adolf Hitler a laurel wreath from the sacred grove at Olympia, the site of the ancient Olympics. He died in 1940.

Memorable marathon moments

The marathon has rarely been short of drama. In 1904 at St Louis, Zulu tribesman Lentauw (one of the first two black Africans to compete in the Olympics) was chased off the course and through a cornfield by dogs. He still finished ninth.

The 1908 London marathon began at Windsor Castle and ended in the Olympic stadium at Shepherd's Bush – a distance of 26 miles. The runners then had to push themselves through another 385 yards around the track – so that the finishing line would be right in front of Queen Alexandra's royal box! But in all but two of the Games since then, the official marathon distance has been set at 26 miles 385 yards (or about 42 kilometres).

In 1960 Rome staged the first night marathon, since the daytime heat was just too great. Both that race and the 1964 marathon were won by Ethiopian Abebe Bikila The first man into the stadium at Munich in 1972 was American Frank Shorter. To his surprise all he heard was whistling and booing. But he was not the target. Shortly before, a hoaxer had appeared on the track and run a full lap before security guards closed in on him. The crowd was still jeering *him*.

In Barcelona in 1992, Mongolian Pyambuu Tuul recorded a time of 4 hours and 44 seconds – the slowest in 84 years. But Tuul had been blinded by an explosion in 1978, then in 1990 he had run in the New York marathon with a guide's help. A year later an operation gave him partial sight, so he entered for the Barcelona Olympics – not to win but 'to show that a man has many possibilities'.

The winner of the third-ever women's marathon, at Barcelona in 1992, was Russia's Valentina Yegorova. Hundreds of friends and neighbours back in her farming village of Iziderkino bought a 30-year-old TV set and crowded around it in the street to watch her take the gold.

Which sports?

How many different Olympic sports can you name? It can be tempting to think only of athletics, gymnastics and swimming. Those sports certainly attract more media coverage than most, but they are just the tip of the iceberg. At the 26th Olympic Games of 1996, in Atlanta, the competitors took part in 26 different sports. The box below shows what they were. World-class facilities have to be provided for all of them, so you can see how big a job it is for a modern-day host city to stage an Olympic Games.

Olympic sports featured in Atlanta, 1996

Archery
Athletics
Basketball
Beach Volleyball
Boxing
Canoeing
Canoe Slalom
Cycling
Equestrianism

Fencing
Freestyle Wrestling
Greco-Roman Wrestling
Gymnastics
Handball
Hockey
Judo
Modern **Pentathlon**
Rowing

Shooting
Soccer
Swimming
Table Tennis
Tennis
Volleyball
Weightlifting
Yachting

At Sydney in the year 2000 the number will rise again, with the addition of Triathlon and Tae kwon do.

Canoeing: a fiercely contested Olympic sport. Kayak events feature paddles with a blade at each end. The paddles in Canadian canoeing have only one blade.

The International Olympic Committee's Programme Commission constantly discusses Olympic sports which already exist, and possible new ones for the future. Some sports fans around the world were not sure if Beach Volleyball was quite 'serious' enough to be added to the programme in Atlanta. But, at various Games since 1896, many sports have tried and failed to find a permanent place in the Olympics. The box shows the sports that now belong to the mists of Olympic history.

Discontinued Olympic sports

(Years in brackets show when they were staged)

Cricket (1900) Britain won – beating a French team made up mostly of Englishmen!

Croquet (1900) France won all three croquet events.

Golf (1900, 1904) In 1904 Canadian joker George Lyon became Olympic champion – and accepted a silver trophy after walking down the path to the ceremony on his hands.

Jeu de Paume – 'Real Tennis' (1908) American Jay Gould won gold.

Lacrosse (1904, 1908) In 1908, when Frank Dixon of Canada broke his stick, British opponent R G W Martin offered to withdraw from the game until a new one was found. The Canadians went on to win the Olympic final.

Motorboating (1908) Briton Thomas Thornycroft won gold in two different classes. 44 years later, aged 70, he was selected for the British yachting team at the 1952 Helsinki Games.

Polo (1900, 1908, 1920, 1924, 1936) In the last competition, Argentina won gold in front of a crowd of 45,000 people.

Racquets (1908) Britain won a clean sweep of all the medals.

Roque – hard-surface croquet (1904) A clean sweep for the USA.

Rugby union (1900, 1908, 1920, 1924) Team-member Daniel Carroll won gold for Australia in 1908 and then for the USA in 1920. No one else has ever won gold medals for representing different countries.

Tug-of-war (1900, 1904, 1908, 1912, 1920) The first team to pull the other for six feet was declared the winner. In 1908 teams of British policemen came first, second and third.

Olympic rituals

Processions and parades took place at the ancient Greek Games and now they are dramatic features of the modern Olympics. Each new opening ceremony – watched by enormous TV audiences – seems to outdo the last for spectacular entertainments and effects. The procession of competitors is still led by Greece, followed by all the other national teams in alphabetical order, with the host country's team appearing last. In Melbourne in 1956, a seventeen-year-old Chinese boy suggested that everyone should walk together as a single **multicultural** nation at the Games' closing ceremony – it made a wonderful sight.

At Barcelona, Spain, in 1992, a crowd of 100,000 people and a TV audience of two billion watched one of the most breathtaking opening ceremonies ever.

The Olympic oath

'In the name of all competitors, I promise that we will take part in these Olympic Games, respecting and abiding by the rules which govern them, in the true spirit of sportsmanship, for the glory of sport and the honour of our teams.'

Since 1920, a representative of the host country has taken this oath at the opening ceremony of each Games. Usually the oath-taker is a veteran of previous Games: like Finnish gymnast Heikki Savolainen at Helsinki in 1952 and Korean basketball player Hur Jae at Seoul in 1988.

Mascots

The first Olympic mascot made its appearance at Mexico City in 1968: a red jaguar. Since then each Games has had its own named mascot – usually chosen because of a connection with the host country. Popular mascots have included Misha the Bear at Moscow in 1980, Waldi the Dachshund at Munich in 1972 and Cobi the Dog at Barcelona in 1992. Since 1980 the Winter Games have had mascots too.

Tending the flame

At Amsterdam in 1928 the Olympic flame was first lit, and it burned throughout the Games. Eight years later, the first 'torch relay' was run: with 3000 runners bringing the 'sacred fire' 3000 kilometres from Olympia, where the Sun's rays ignited it, to Berlin. In 1956, for the Melbourne Games, the torch first travelled by air. 20 years later, the flame's energy sent a laser beam from Greece to Montreal – and lit an identical torch! Then at Atlanta in 1996, there was a moving moment when ex-Olympic champion boxer Muhammad Ali – now a sufferer from **Parkinson's disease** – lit the Olympic flame in his own country.

Since 1920 this has been the official Olympic flag. It was designed by the founder of the modern Games, Baron de Coubertin. The coloured rings are nowadays believed to represent the five continents of the world, linked together by sport. These five colours were chosen because, in 1920, at least one of them appeared in the flag of each participating country.

Medal ceremonies

In ancient Greece, all the Olympic winners were presented with olive wreaths at the end of the Games. At each modern Games until 1928, victors' medals were also given out at the closing ceremony. Now medals are presented to the winners of each event as it takes place. (Incidentally, Olympic gold medals are 90 per cent solid silver, with 6 grams of gold on top.)

The podium or victory stand – with its 1-2-3 positions – was introduced in 1932. Some people think national anthems should not be played at Olympic medal presentations. After all, the Games are meant to be *inter*national. At Tokyo in 1964, when Abebe Bikila received Ethiopia's first-ever gold medal, the Japanese band did not know the Ethiopian anthem – so it played Japan's anthem instead!

Men only?

In ancient times very few women were allowed to watch Olympic events. No women *at all* were allowed to take part in them. When the modern Games began in 1896, there were still no women competitors. Many people believed that women's bodies could not cope with the demands of top-level sport. Some thought, too, that a woman's true place was in the home, not the stadium.

Times change, and so do people's ideas. The table shows how the number of female Olympians has risen over the past 100 years – until at Atlanta in 1996, 3513 women took part. That figure is still some way short of the 6797 male participants, but the gap is now closing all the time.

Women admitted at last

The earliest female Olympians were golfers and tennis players. American Margaret Abbott won a golfing gold medal at a Paris tournament in 1900, without even realizing that she was taking part in the Olympic Games!

MALE AND FEMALE COMPETITORS AT THE SUMMER OLYMPICS			
Year	Venue	Men	Women
1896	Athens	245	–
1900	Paris	1206	19
1904	St Louis	681	6
1908	London	1999	36
1912	Stockholm	2490	57
1920	Antwerp	2591	78
1924	Paris	2956	136
1928	Amsterdam	2724	290
1932	Los Angeles	1281	127
1936	Berlin	3738	328
1948	London	3714	385
1952	Helsinki	4407	518
1956	Melbourne	2958	384
1960	Rome	4738	610
1964	Tokyo	4457	683
1968	Mexico City	4750	781
1972	Munich	6065	1058
1976	Montreal	4781	1247
1980	Moscow	4092	1125
1984	Los Angeles	5230	1567
1988	Seoul	6279	2186
1992	Barcelona	6659	2708
1996	Atlanta	6797	3513

The first Olympic marathon for women was staged in Los Angeles in 1984. It was won by American Joan Benoit in a time of 2 hrs 24 mins 52 secs. That was quite an improvement on the first official, pre-Olympic time clocked by a female marathon runner – 3 hrs 40 mins 22 secs by Violet Piercy of Great Britain in 1926. (Even so, Piercy's record stood unchallenged for 37 years!)

Women made their debut in Olympic **track and field** events at Amsterdam in 1928. For the first time they competed in 100 metres races, the 400 metres relay, the discus and high jump. They also took part in 800 metres races, but several runners were seen to be 'in distress' at the end of a hard final and another 44 years passed before a longer women's race – the 1500 metres – was added to the programme. And it was not until 1984 that women were allowed to compete in the most gruelling Olympic race of all – the marathon.

A woman called Babe

One woman who did more than most for the cause of female Olympians was Mildred 'Babe' Didrikson. At the Los Angeles Games in 1932, this confident eighteen-year-old American announced: 'I came out here to beat everybody in sight, and that is exactly what I'm going to do.' She proceeded to win the javelin and broke the world record to win the 80 metres hurdles. In the high jump, she tied for first place and claimed another world record, but received only a silver medal because an official had called her head-first 'diving' style illegal. She would doubtless have won more gold, but women then were allowed to compete in only three events – even though Babe had qualified for five. In later life she excelled in basketball and golf. Someone once asked if there was anything she did not play. 'Yeah,' she replied. 'Dolls'.

Babe Didrikson, heroine of 1932.

For the love of sport

Amateurs are meant to play sport purely for the love of it. **Professionals** receive material rewards. Nowadays almost all Olympic competitors are professionals; even top soccer players are allowed to take part. Sporting standards are so high that few athletes could train to the right level *and* do regular jobs. Yet that was what the organizers of the first modern Games wanted them to do. And, until quite recent times, amateurism remained the Olympic ideal.

A noble tradition

'The important thing in the Olympic Games is not winning but taking part. The essential thing in life is not conquering but fighting well.' Baron de Coubertin and his fellow-organizers of the first modern Games believed very strongly in this point of view. For them, simply taking part was its own reward. Certainly there was no question of money being paid – either as a prize for the winners of events, or to competitors as expenses for their training programmes. Olympic sport was thus a glorious hobby for those who could afford to take part.

But the line between amateur and professional in Olympic sport was never completely clear. Spiridon Louis won the first marathon in 1896, and received a simple laurel wreath for his achievement. But his fans also promised him a multitude of gifts, including free groceries, free travel and free haircuts for life! 'Material rewards' like these *did* sometimes go to the victors.

Sport today is an expensive business. Worldwide sports sponsorship by business companies helps to pay the costs.

Olympic athletes were once meant to be amateurs. But by 1974 National Olympic Committees were allowed to pay athletes while in full-time training, and in 1981 **track and field** athletes were allowed to receive money for endorsing products, like the running shoe shown in the picture.

Paralympic progress

In the first part of the modern Olympic era, there was no place for competitors who loved sport but were disabled. This seemed unfortunate to Sir Ludwig Guttman, who went on to become the founder of the 'Paralympics'.

In 1948 Guttman was director of the National Spinal Injuries Centre at Stoke Mandeville Hospital in England. His original idea was to hold competitive sports for people with spinal injuries, in Britain at the Stoke Mandeville Games. But year by year people with other disabilities and from other nations got involved, and in 1960 a four-yearly 'parallel Olympics' for handicapped sportsmen and women began. In that year 400 athletes competed at Rome. By 1996 in Atlanta the number was closer to 4000. The Games are now usually held in the ten days or so following the main Olympic Games.

The range of sports staged at the Paralympics in recent times is quite awesome: from table tennis to baseball and basketball – and even team rhythmic gymnastics. After the Barcelona Games where Tanni Grey (see right) was such a star, the British *Sunday Times* reported: 'The stadium was on several occasions packed with up to 55,000 people who had not come to be "nice to the disabled" … but to see athletics of the highest calibre.'

This is Tanni Grey from Wales. At the Barcelona Paralympics in 1992 she won four gold medals for Britain – in the 100 m, 200 m, 400 m and 800 m: a personal tally beaten only by Bart Dodson of the USA.

Ice-cold Olympics

Figure skating featured in the Olympic Games of 1908 and 1920, and ice hockey too was played in 1920. But in 1924 the International Olympic Committee established a completely separate Winter Olympic Games. From then until 1992, they were always staged in the same year as the Summer Games, although not always in the same country (see Table). But beginning with the 1994 Games at Lillehammer, the Winter Olympics were rescheduled to take place in the even-numbered years that fell between the Summer Games. In the 1924 Games at St Moritz, there were fourteen events in five different sports. At Nagano in 1998 there were 67, and the new Olympic sports there included curling and women's ice hockey.

WHERE THE WINTER OLYMPICS HAVE BEEN HELD:

1924 Chamonix, France
1928 St Moritz, Switzerland
1932 Lake Placid, USA
1936 Garmisch-Partenkirchen, Germany
1948 St Moritz, Switzerland
1952 Oslo, Norway
1956 Cortina, Italy
1960 Squaw Valley, USA
1964 Innsbruck, Austria
1968 Grenoble, France
1972 Sapporo, Japan
1976 Innsbruck, Austria
1980 Lake Placid, USA
1984 Sarajevo, Yugoslavia (now Bosnia)
1988 Calgary, Canada
1992 Albertville, France
1994 Lillehammer, Norway
1998 Nagano, Japan

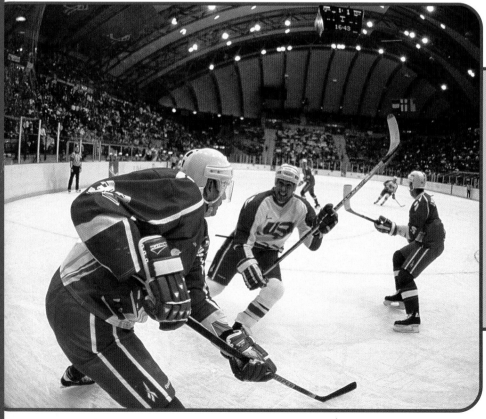

An exciting moment from the ice-hockey match between France and the USA at the Lillehammer Winter Olympics in 1994. In the final, Sweden beat Canada to win gold.

Snow joke

Far fewer countries send teams to the Winter Games than to the Summer. Poor countries with warm climates can rarely afford, for example, to construct ice rinks in which to train up future champions. (But at Albertville in 1992, there *was*, believe it or not, a four-man bobsleigh team from Jamaica!) The mountainous countries of Europe have dominated the vast majority of the eighteen Games. Norway, the **USSR**, Sweden, Switzerland and Germany have been especially successful in the final medals tables.

Often the Winter Olympians have to compete against the weather as well as one another. Rain, thaw, blizzard and gale have all been problems – and in 1964 at Innsbruck, after a very mild winter, there was simply not enough snow for the Alpine skiing. Austrian troops had to transport over 25,000 tonnes of the powdery stuff to the River Inn valley from higher snowfields!

Alpine skiing for both men and women is divided into five separate events: downhill, slalom, giant slalom, super-giant slalom and alpine combination (downhill and slalom). Here Luxembourg's Marc Girardelli is competing in the downhill at the Lillehammer Winter Olympics.

SPORTS FEATURED AT THE NAGANO WINTER OLYMPICS OF 1998

Alpine skiing
Biathlon
Bobsleigh
Curling
Figure skating
Ice hockey

Lugeing
Nordic skiing
Short-track speed skating
Snowboarding
Speed skating
Trick skiing

Glossary

aggression warlike or hostile act

amateur someone who competes for fun, rather than as a job, and who is unpaid

apartheid policy of keeping black people apart from, and inferior to, whites

aristocrat a member of the upper or privileged classes

boycott to refuse to have anything to do with a person, country or event

Cold War period, after World War Two, of unfriendly relations between the USA and the USSR, which never quite became real warfare

commercialization attempt to make money from something

Communist the idea that a single, ruling political party can provide for all its people better than if they are left to make their own decisions and keep their own homes, land and businesses. The USSR became the first Communist state in 1917. After World War Two, the USSR introduced Communism into much of eastern Europe.

defect leave one country to live in another, without official permission

delegate someone sent to a meeting as a representative of another person or group of people

eco-friendly in harmony with the natural environment

equestrianism riding or performing on horseback

landfill area of land filled in by rubbish or waste material

multicultural to do with people who come from different countries and have different ideas

Nazi short form of the National Socialist German Workers' Party, a political party led by Adolf Hitler

Parkinson's disease illness that affects a person's nerves

pentathlon athletic contest where a competitor takes part in five different events

professional paid competitor

public school (in Britain) school which charges fees from parents

reclaim make land useful or productive

taxpayer person who pays a portion of their earnings to the government to pay for the running of the country

terrorist someone who uses violence to force a government to do what he or she wants

track and field sporting events which involve running, jumping, throwing and walking – such as the 100 metres or the javelin

truce temporary halting of a war or fight

USSR a Communist country, including Russia and many smaller nations, which broke up in 1991

Index